UNVEILING THE PAST

A JOURNEY THROUGH ARCHAEOLOGY

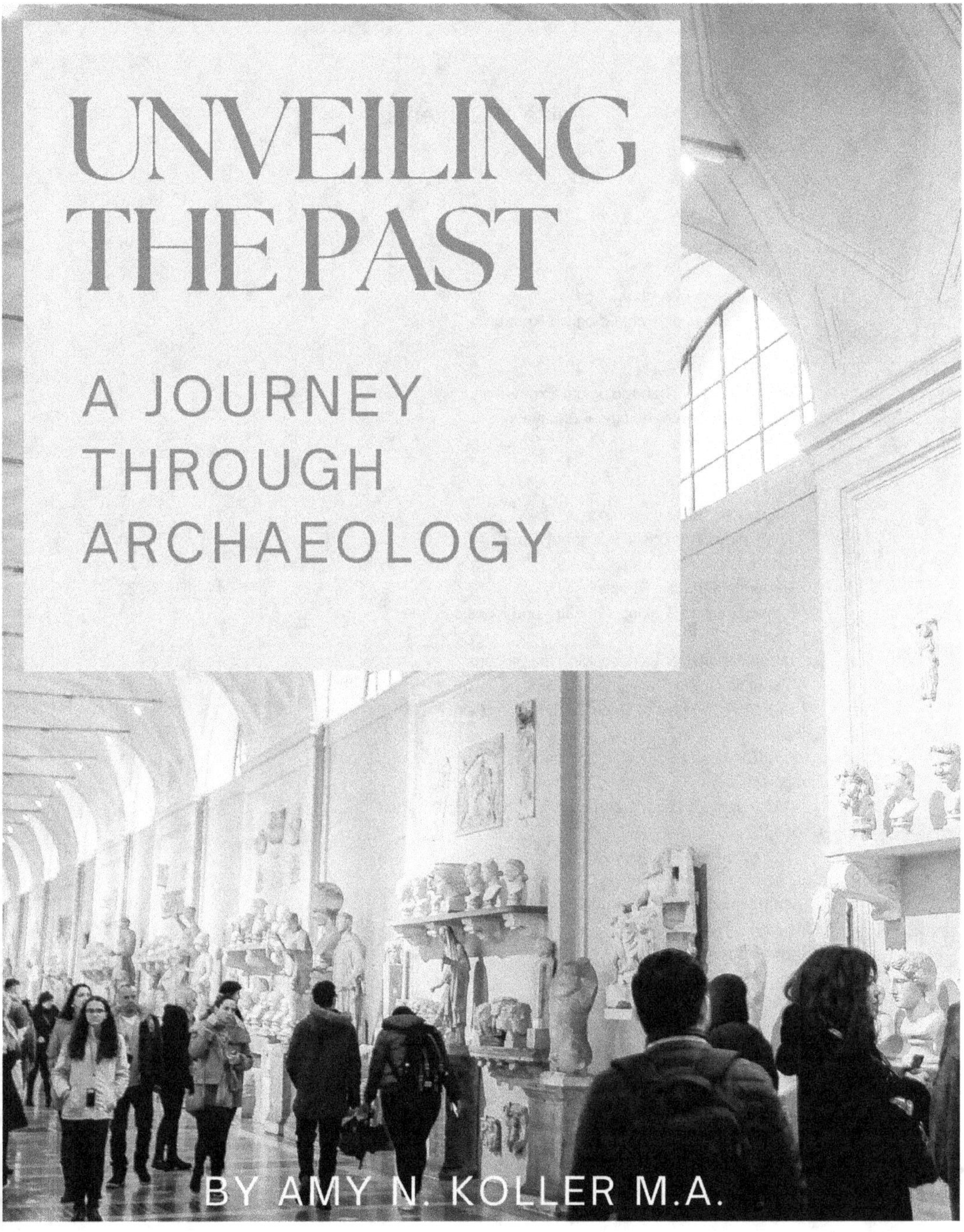

BY AMY N. KOLLER M.A.

Table of Contents

Chapter 1

The Essence of Archaeology

Archaeology is a fascinating field that allows us to uncover and understand the lives of ancient civilizations and cultures. This book will take you on a captivating journey through the world of archaeology, exploring its methods, discoveries, and significance.

So, what exactly is archaeology? Archaeology is a multidisciplinary field of study that focuses on the investigation, analysis, and interpretation of past human cultures and societies through the examination of physical remains, artifacts, structures, and landscapes. It aims to reconstruct and understand the history, behavior, technology, beliefs, and social interactions of ancient civilizations and peoples.

Archaeologists use a variety of methods and techniques, such as excavation, surveying, dating methods (such as radiocarbon dating and stratigraphy), artifact analysis, and comparative studies, to piece together a comprehensive understanding of the past. By examining material remains like pottery, tools, architecture, human remains, and other artifacts, archaeologists gain insights into how societies evolved, adapted, and interacted with their environment over time.

The field of archaeology can encompass a wide range of time periods and geographical locations, from prehistoric times to more recent historical eras. It contributes to our understanding of human history, cultural evolution, and the development of societies, shedding light on both well-known civilizations and lesser-known communities that have left their mark on the archaeological record. Archaeology, history, and anthropology are related disciplines that focus on understanding human societies and cultures, but they have distinct methodologies, approaches, and emphases.

Archaeology

Archaeology is the study of past human cultures and societies through the analysis of material remains such as artifacts, structures, and landscapes. It aims to reconstruct and understand the lives, behaviors, and practices of ancient societies by examining the physical evidence they left behind. Archaeologists often excavate and analyze artifacts, bones, tools, buildings, and other remnants to piece together the story of a particular culture or time period.

Key Features of Archaeology:

- Focuses on Material Culture: Archaeologists primarily study physical objects and their context to understand past societies.

- Inferences from Artifacts: Interpretations are based on analyzing artifacts' design, technology, style, and context.

- Emphasis on Context: The spatial relationships between artifacts and their surroundings are crucial for understanding their significance.

- Limited to Prehistoric and Historic Periods: Archaeology typically deals with periods before written records or in conjunction with historical records.

History

History is the study of past events and human activities based on written records, documents, and oral traditions. Historians analyze texts, documents, and narratives to reconstruct the past and provide insights into the actions, motivations, and cultural developments of societies. History focuses on interpreting and narrating events as well as understanding the broader social, political, and cultural contexts in which they occurred.

Key Features of History:

- Relies on Written Records: Historians primarily use written sources to reconstruct past events and societies.

- Narrative and Interpretation: The focus is on constructing a chronological account of events and interpreting their significance.

- Emphasis on Human Experiences: History often aims to understand the thoughts, motivations, and emotions of historical figures.

- Access to Recent History: History can cover periods with written records, extending into more recent times.

Anthropology

Anthropology is the holistic study of human societies and cultures. It encompasses various subfields, including *cultural anthropology, linguistic anthropology, biological anthropology,* and archaeology. While archaeology is a subfield of anthropology, the distinction lies in the fact that anthropology as a whole examines contemporary societies and cultures, often involving direct interaction and ethnographic research. Anthropologists study human behavior, social structures, language, and biological adaptations, seeking to understand the diversity of human experiences across time and space.

Key Features of Anthropology:

- **_Holistic Approach:_** Anthropology examines various aspects of human societies, including cultural, linguistic, and biological dimensions.

- **_Contemporary and Historical Focus:_** Anthropology encompasses the study of both modern and past cultures, using methods such as ethnography and participant observation.

- **_Cross-Cultural Comparisons:_** Anthropologists aim to identify commonalities and differences among different societies to understand the breadth of human variation.

In summary, while archaeology, history, and anthropology share a common goal of understanding human cultures and societies, they differ in their primary sources of evidence, methodologies, and time frames. Archaeology relies on material remains, history focuses on written records, and anthropology takes a broader, holistic approach that includes both contemporary and past cultures.

Primary Goals of Archaeological Research

Archaeological research aims to uncover and understand the past by studying material remains left behind by ancient societies and cultures. The field of archaeology has several key goals, and reconstructing past societies, cultures, and lifestyles is a central aspect of this endeavor. Archaeologists strive to piece together the social structures, hierarchies, and organization of past societies. By analyzing artifacts, architecture, and other material remains, they can infer how people lived, interacted, and organized themselves within their cultural contexts.

Archaeology helps us track the development and evolution of technologies over time. Through the study of tools, implements, and other artifacts, researchers can deduce how ancient cultures adapted to their environments and improved their ways of life through technological innovations. Archaeological research sheds light on the gradual changes and transformations within cultures over extended periods. By analyzing artifacts, art, and architecture from different time periods, researchers can identify shifts in religious beliefs, artistic styles, economic systems, and more.

Understanding the economic activities of past societies is a critical aspect of archaeological research. Analysis of trade networks, agricultural practices, production techniques, and consumption patterns can provide insights into how people sustained themselves and interacted with neighboring regions. Archaeologists are interested in the everyday lives of people in the past. By studying artifacts related to food, clothing, housing, personal adornment, and other aspects of daily life, researchers can reconstruct how individuals from various social strata lived and interacted.

Archaeological research contributes to the preservation and interpretation of cultural heritage. By documenting and conserving archaeological sites, artifacts, and structures, researchers ensure that the knowledge and history of past cultures are preserved for future generations. Archaeological findings provide valuable data that can complement written historical records. In many cases, archaeological evidence helps corroborate, challenge, or fill gaps in historical narratives, leading to a more comprehensive understanding of the past.

Archaeology often involves collaboration with various scientific disciplines, such as anthropology, history, geology, chemistry, and more. This multidisciplinary approach allows researchers to gather diverse perspectives and draw accurate conclusions about the past. Archaeological research also extends to the study of human evolution. The examination of ancient hominin remains and associated artifacts helps scientists piece together the evolutionary journey of our species and its adaptations over time.

Archaeological research can have implications for contemporary issues, such as cultural heritage management, indigenous rights, and sustainable development. By studying how past societies interacted with their environments, modern societies can learn valuable lessons for addressing present-day challenges. The primary goal of archaeological research is to reconstruct and understand the complexities of past societies, cultures, and lifestyles. This knowledge not only enriches our understanding of history but also offers insights into human adaptation, innovation, and resilience across different time periods and geographic regions.

Chapter 2

Unearthing the Past

Excavation is a fundamental and primary method of archaeological investigation used to uncover and study the remains of past human activities and cultures. It involves the systematic and controlled removal of soil and other materials from archaeological sites to reveal artifacts, features, and structures that have been buried over time. Excavation plays a crucial role in understanding the chronology, spatial layout, and social contexts of ancient societies, offering insights into their lifestyles, technologies, and behaviors.

Key Aspects of Archaeological Excavation

Site Selection and Preparation

Archaeologists choose excavation sites based on various criteria, such as historical significance, research objectives, and the potential for discovering well-preserved remains. Before excavation begins, thorough planning, including research, surveying, and mapping, is carried out to establish a clear understanding of the site's layout and potential.

Stratigraphy

One of the core principles of excavation is the concept of stratigraphy, which involves studying the layers of sediment or soil that accumulate over time. These layers, or "strata," are often indicative of different periods of occupation or activity. By carefully excavating each layer, archaeologists can create a chronological sequence of events and artifacts.

Excavation Techniques

Excavation techniques vary depending on the nature of the site and the research goals. Tools such as trowels, brushes, shovels, and even small hand-held implements are used to delicately remove soil and uncover artifacts. The process is slow and meticulous to avoid damaging fragile materials.

Recording and Documentation

Accurate recording and documentation are critical during excavation. Archaeologists document the location, orientation, and context of each artifact, feature, and layer. Precise measurements, photographs, sketches, and notes are taken to ensure a comprehensive record of the site.

Artifact Recovery

As excavation progresses, artifacts such as pottery, tools, jewelry, and bones are discovered. These objects provide insights into the daily lives, beliefs, and technologies of past societies. Each artifact's position and association with specific layers or features are carefully recorded.

Feature Identification

Apart from individual artifacts, archaeological features like hearths, walls, pits, and post holes are also uncovered. These features provide information about the architecture, activities, and structures of the past.

Environmental Analysis

Soil samples, pollen, seeds, and other organic materials collected during excavation are subjected to environmental analysis. These studies can provide information about the local environment, diet, and subsistence practices of ancient people.

Dating Techniques

Excavation allows archaeologists to establish relative and absolute dating through stratigraphy and scientific techniques like radiocarbon dating. This helps create a chronological framework for the site's history.

Interpretation and Analysis

After excavation, archaeologists analyze the collected data to construct a narrative of the site's history and the people who inhabited it. The context, spatial relationships, and artifact assemblages contribute to understanding ancient societies and their activities.

Publication and Preservation

Excavation reports and scholarly publications communicate the findings, interpretations, and methodologies employed during excavation. Additionally, the preservation of excavated materials is vital to ensure that future generations of researchers can reexamine and reinterpret the evidence using advanced technologies and methodologies.

Excavation is a dynamic process that requires a combination of scientific rigor, attention to detail, and a deep understanding of archaeological theory and methods. It forms the backbone of archaeological research, allowing us to uncover and reconstruct the rich tapestry of human history.

Archaeological excavation is a meticulous process that involves uncovering and studying artifacts, structures, and other remains from the past to understand human history and culture. The following is a step-by-step explanation of the process, from site selection to documentation:

Site Selection

Archaeologists begin by selecting a site for excavation. This choice is based on various factors, including historical records, aerial surveys, remote sensing techniques, and sometimes even local folklore. The site's potential to yield valuable information about the past, its historical significance, and its accessibility are key considerations.

Survey and Mapping

Before excavating, a preliminary survey is conducted. This may involve walking the site to identify surface artifacts, features, and potential excavation areas. Mapping and documenting the site's layout, including visible features and topography, help in planning the excavation strategy.

Excavation Strategy

Archaeologists develop an excavation plan that outlines the research questions they aim to address and the methods they will employ. This plan considers the site's historical context, potential stratigraphy (layering of soil and materials), and the types of artifacts or features expected to be found.

Setting Up the Grid

The excavation area is divided into a grid system using strings, ropes, or physical markers. Each square of the grid is typically assigned a unique identifier for recording purposes.

Initial Testing

The excavation begins with small test pits or trenches to explore the layers of soil and establish the site's stratigraphy. Archaeologists carefully remove soil layer by layer, documenting any artifacts or features encountered.

Actual Excavation

After testing, the main excavation process begins. Layers are removed systematically, with each layer being documented before removal. Archaeologists use various tools such as trowels, brushes, and sometimes even dental tools to carefully uncover artifacts and features.

Artifact Recovery

Recovered artifacts are cleaned, cataloged, and labeled with precise information about their location, layer, and context. Important data like material, size, shape, and any associated artifacts or features are recorded.

Stratigraphic Analysis

Layers of soil and artifacts are analyzed in terms of their relative dating and chronology. This helps establish a timeline of human activity at the site.

Feature Documentation

Structural remains, hearths, pits, and other features are meticulously recorded through measurements, drawings, and photography.

Environmental Sampling

Soil samples are collected for analysis of pollen, plant remains, and other environmental indicators that provide insights into past landscapes and human activities.

Contextual Analysis
Artifacts, features, and layers are analyzed in relation to one another to understand their cultural and historical context. Interpretation involves linking findings to historical records and existing knowledge.

Data Interpretation
All collected data is analyzed to answer research questions and develop interpretations about the site's history, the people who lived there, and their activities.

Publication and Preservation
The findings, analyses, and interpretations are compiled into reports, articles, or monographs for academic and public dissemination. Artifacts are conserved, and the site might be backfilled and preserved for future research or public education.

Public Outreach
Archaeologists often engage in public outreach and education to share their findings and promote awareness of the site's historical importance.

In each step of the process, meticulous attention to detail, precise documentation, and collaboration among archaeologists and specialists are crucial to ensure accurate and meaningful results from the excavation.

Key Tools of Archaeological Excavation

Archaeological excavation is a meticulous process that involves the careful removal of layers of soil and sediment to uncover artifacts, structures, and other remains from the past. Various tools are employed to ensure that artifacts are handled with care, contexts are preserved, and important information is gathered. Here's a discussion of some of the key tools used in archaeological excavation:

Trowels
Trowels are one of the most essential tools in an archaeologist's toolkit. They come in various shapes and sizes, but a common design is a pointed or squared-off blade attached to a handle. Trowels are used to carefully remove soil layer by layer, allowing archaeologists to distinguish different layers and features. The pointed end is particularly useful for detailed work, while the flat end is used for larger-scale excavation.

Brushes

Brushes are used to gently remove loose dirt and sediment from artifacts, surfaces, and features. Soft-bristled brushes prevent damage to fragile materials. Brushes also help reveal fine details and distinguish characteristics of artifacts and structures without causing harm.

Shovels and Picks
Larger excavation areas or particularly dense soils may require the use of shovels and picks. These tools are used to remove larger quantities of soil quickly, but they are generally avoided in sensitive areas to prevent inadvertent damage.

Screens, Sieves or Sifters
Screens (also commonly referred to as sieves or sifters) are used to separate smaller artifacts, organic materials, and debris from soil. The soil is placed into the sieve, which is then shaken or agitated. This process allows archaeologists to recover smaller items that might have been missed during excavation.

Dental Picks and Small Tools
Dental picks, scalpels, and other small precision tools are used for intricate excavation work. They are particularly useful when working on delicate artifacts, cleaning intricate details, or separating artifacts from adhering soil.

Pliers and Tweezers
Pliers and tweezers are employed to handle delicate artifacts and materials, such as small bones, beads, and other fragile items. They allow for precise manipulation without causing damage.

Measuring and Recording Tools
Archaeologists use measuring tapes, rulers, and other measurement tools to record the precise location and depth of artifacts and features within the excavation grid. This information is crucial for creating accurate site maps and reconstructing the spatial relationships between artifacts.

Levels and Plumb Bobs
Levels and plumb bobs help ensure that excavated features are properly aligned and oriented. This is crucial for maintaining accuracy in recording and interpreting the positions of artifacts and structures.

Water Sprayers
Water sprayers are used to dampen the soil during excavation, helping to prevent the soil from crumbling excessively. This can be particularly useful when working with delicate features or in dry, arid conditions.

Photography and Documentation Tools
Cameras and other documentation tools are essential for capturing images of the excavation process, artifacts, and features. Photography is crucial for creating a detailed record of the excavation process and for later analysis.

Personal Protective Equipment (PPE)
Depending on the excavation site and the potential presence of hazardous materials, archaeologists may use PPE such as gloves, masks, goggles, and even full suits to protect themselves and prevent cross-contamination.

It's important to note that different archaeological sites and contexts may require specialized tools or variations of these tools to suit specific needs. The careful selection and use of tools are crucial to ensure that artifacts and contextual information are preserved and that the excavation process is conducted responsibly and ethically.

Careful stratigraphy and context preservation are essential principles in archaeology that play a crucial role in accurately interpreting archaeological findings and reconstructing the past. They provide a framework for understanding the relationships between artifacts, features, and layers of sediment in an archaeological site. Here is why these principles are so important:

Chronological Understanding: *Stratigraphy* involves the study of layers of sediment or soil that accumulate over time. These layers represent different periods of human activity. By carefully excavating and documenting these layers, archaeologists can establish a chronological sequence of events. This chronological understanding is vital for constructing accurate timelines and understanding the development of a site over time.

Contextual Information: The context in which an artifact or feature is found is critical for its interpretation. Context includes the spatial relationships between artifacts and features within a layer, as well as their vertical position within the stratigraphy. This information provides insights into how people used and interacted with their surroundings. For instance, the location of a ceramic vessel within a household context can reveal its function and significance.

Activity Reconstruction: Careful stratigraphic excavation allows archaeologists to identify different activity areas within a site. By analyzing the distribution of artifacts and features across layers, researchers can infer the types of activities that took place in different parts of the site. This can lead to a more accurate reconstruction of past human behavior, such as subsistence practices, trade, and social interactions.

Preservation of Associations: Context preservation ensures that artifacts and features are kept in their original positions until they are properly documented and analyzed. This preserves associations between different artifacts and features, which can provide valuable information about their use, meaning, and significance. Disrupting these associations through careless excavation can lead to the loss of crucial data.

Cultural Interpretation: Understanding the cultural context of archaeological findings is key to interpreting their significance. Stratigraphy and context preservation enable archaeologists to differentiate between different cultural phases, identify changes in material culture, and detect cultural interactions or transitions. This information helps researchers draw more accurate conclusions about the people who inhabited the site.

Site Formation Processes: Stratigraphy and context preservation also shed light on the processes that shaped the archaeological site over time. Natural processes like erosion, sediment deposition, and human activities like construction and abandonment can be deciphered from the layers. This knowledge is vital for distinguishing between artifacts and features that were originally part of the same context and those that might have been introduced later.

Careful stratigraphy and context preservation are fundamental to accurate archaeological interpretation. They provide the tools needed to reconstruct past activities, understand cultural dynamics, and create reliable narratives about human history. Without these principles, archaeological findings risk losing their context and becoming isolated artifacts with limited interpretive value.

Chapter 3

Beyond the Dirt

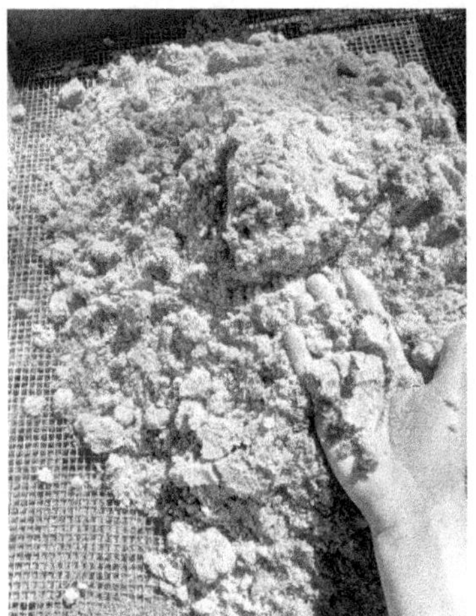

Archaeological laboratory techniques play a crucial role in the proper documentation, analysis, and preservation of artifacts and other archaeological materials recovered from excavation sites. These techniques help researchers uncover valuable insights about past cultures, technologies, and environments.

Once artifacts are excavated, they often require thorough cleaning to remove dirt, debris, and corrosion. This process helps reveal their original features and details. Cleaning methods vary depending on the material type, fragility, and level of preservation. Techniques may include brushing, gentle scraping, micro-excavation with dental tools, and controlled water washing. It's important to use non-destructive methods to avoid damaging the artifacts.

Conservation involves stabilizing and preserving artifacts to prevent further deterioration. This is especially important for delicate or fragile materials that might be susceptible to environmental factors. Common conservation techniques include:

- **Desalination:** Removing salts from artifacts like metals and ceramics to prevent corrosion.
- **Consolidation:** Strengthening fragile materials using adhesives or consolidants.
- **Humidity Control:** Storing artifacts in controlled environments to prevent mold growth, cracking, and warping.
- **Documentation:** Recording the conservation process in detail to ensure the integrity of the artifact's history.

Analyzing artifacts in the laboratory involves examining their physical, chemical, and structural characteristics to gain insights into their origins, uses, and cultural significance. Different techniques are used for various types of artifacts:

- **Ceramics Analysis:** Involves typology (classifying based on shape and style), petrography (studying the mineral composition), and residue analysis (detecting remnants of food, plants, or other substances).

- **Lithics Analysis:** Focuses on stone tools, including their raw materials, manufacturing techniques, and use-wear patterns.
- **Metals Analysis:** Involves metallurgical analysis to determine alloy composition, craftsmanship, and evidence of smelting or forging.
- **Organic Material Analysis:** Techniques like pollen analysis, phytolith analysis, and DNA analysis help identify plant remains, ancient diets, and environmental conditions.
- *Zooarchaeology:* Analyzing animal bones to understand past human interactions with animals, diet, and hunting strategies.
- **Dating Techniques:** Archaeologists use laboratory methods to determine the age of artifacts and archaeological sites. Common dating methods include radiocarbon dating (for organic materials), luminescence dating (for minerals like quartz and feldspar), and dendrochronology (tree-ring dating).
- **Remote Sensing and Imaging:** Advanced imaging technologies, such as X-ray fluorescence (XRF) and computed tomography (CT), allow archaeologists to examine artifacts' internal structures without physically damaging them. Ground-penetrating radar and LiDAR are used for remote site mapping and identifying buried features.
- **Digital Documentation:** 3D scanning and modeling technologies are used to create digital replicas of artifacts, allowing for easier sharing, analysis, and virtual preservation.
- **Data Management:** The use of databases and information management systems helps organize and catalog artifact information, laboratory processes, and analytical results for future research and reference.

Archaeological laboratory techniques encompass a wide range of methods aimed at cleaning, conserving, and analyzing artifacts to reconstruct past human societies and cultures. These techniques are essential for preserving the integrity of archaeological materials and advancing our understanding of the past.

Specialized archaeological methods such as radiocarbon dating, dendrochronology, and seriation play a crucial role in establishing chronologies, understanding historical contexts, and uncovering patterns of cultural change within archaeological sites. For example, *radiocarbon dating*, also known as carbon-14 dating or simply C-14 dating, is a widely used method for determining the age of organic materials. This technique relies on the radioactive decay of carbon-14 isotopes in organic materials like bones, charcoal, and plant remains. Carbon-14 is continuously produced in the atmosphere and is incorporated into living organisms. When an organism dies, the carbon-14 within its tissues begins to decay.

The decay of carbon-14 follows a predictable half-life (approximately 5,730 years). By measuring the ratio of carbon-14 to stable carbon isotopes (carbon-12 and carbon-13) in a sample, archaeologists can estimate the age of the material. Radiocarbon dating is effective for dating materials up to around 50,000 years old and has revolutionized the field of archaeology by providing accurate chronological information.

Another method is *dendrochronology*, or tree-ring dating, is a method that relies on the study of tree rings to establish precise chronological sequences. Trees form annual growth rings, with each ring representing one year of growth. The width and characteristics of these rings are influenced by environmental conditions, such as climate and water availability. By comparing overlapping tree-ring patterns from living trees and ancient wood samples, archaeologists can construct long and accurate chronological sequences. Dendrochronology is particularly effective for dating wooden structures, artifacts, and archaeological sites with preserved wooden materials. It provides highly precise dates and can even offer insights into past climate variations.

Seriation is another relative dating method used to order artifacts and other archaeological materials based on changes in style, form, or other characteristics over time. The underlying principle is that cultural styles tend to change gradually, and objects of similar style are likely to have been produced around the same time. This method is especially useful when absolute dating techniques are unavailable or limited.

Archaeologists create seriation sequences by arranging artifacts from different contexts into a chronological order based on stylistic changes. These sequences can reveal patterns of cultural development, trade interactions, and changes in technology. Seriation can be applied to various artifact types, including pottery, tools, and decorative items.

Radiocarbon dating, dendrochronology, and seriation are specialized archaeological methods that contribute to our understanding of past chronologies, cultural changes, and historical contexts. These methods provide valuable insights into the timelines of human activities and interactions, helping archaeologists piece together the puzzle of our shared history.

Technology such as ground-penetrating radar (GPR) and LiDAR (Light Detection and Ranging) have also gone on to revolutionize archaeological surveying by providing researchers with advanced tools to non-invasively explore and document archaeological sites. These technologies have significantly improved the efficiency, accuracy, and comprehensiveness of archaeological investigations. Here's an explanation of how each of these technologies has contributed to this revolution:

Ground-penetrating radar is a geophysical method that uses radar pulses to image the subsurface. It works by sending electromagnetic pulses into the ground and recording the reflections that bounce back. GPR is particularly useful in archaeological surveying for several reasons:

- **Subsurface Imaging:** GPR can detect buried features, structures, and anomalies beneath the ground's surface without the need for excavation. This allows archaeologists to map the layout of structures, walls, foundations, and even artifacts buried beneath layers of soil.

- **Non-Invasiveness:** GPR is non-destructive, which means it doesn't require physical intervention or excavation to collect valuable data. This is crucial for preserving delicate archaeological sites and minimizing disturbance to artifacts.

- **Time and Cost Efficiency:** Traditional excavation methods can be time-consuming and expensive. GPR accelerates the surveying process by providing a preliminary understanding of a site's layout and potential features, enabling researchers to focus their efforts on specific areas of interest.

- **Mapping and Visualization:** GPR data can be processed to create detailed 2D and 3D maps of the subsurface, allowing archaeologists to visualize the arrangement of structures and artifacts in their original context.

LiDAR is a remote sensing technology that uses laser light to measure distances and create detailed three-dimensional representations of surfaces and objects. In archaeology, LiDAR has proven to be transformative in several ways:

- **Aerial Surveying:** LiDAR can be mounted on aircraft or drones to capture high-resolution topographic data over large areas quickly. This aerial perspective can reveal hidden features, ancient landscapes, and even structures that are not easily visible from the ground.

- **Vegetation Penetration:** LiDAR can penetrate through dense vegetation, allowing archaeologists to see archaeological remains hidden beneath forest canopies or other types of overgrowth.

- **Accuracy and Precision:** LiDAR data is highly accurate and precise, enabling archaeologists to create detailed digital elevation models and 3D visualizations of archaeological sites with sub-centimeter accuracy.

- **Site Discovery:** LiDAR can identify previously unknown archaeological sites, providing researchers with new opportunities for exploration and discovery.

- **Documentation and Conservation:** The high-resolution data generated by LiDAR can serve as a valuable record of archaeological sites, aiding in their documentation and preservation efforts.

Ground-penetrating radar and LiDAR have revolutionized archaeological surveying by allowing researchers to visualize and analyze archaeological sites in ways that were not previously possible. These technologies enable archaeologists to gather information without disturbing the site, to survey large areas efficiently, and to make discoveries that might have otherwise remained hidden.

Chapter 4

Piecing Together the Puzzle

Artifact analysis and interpretation is a crucial aspect of archaeology and cultural anthropology. By studying artifacts, researchers gain insights into past societies, their technologies, beliefs, and ways of life.

Pottery is one of the most common artifacts found at archaeological sites. Analyzing pottery involves examining its composition, style, decoration, and context. Different types of pottery can provide information about trade networks, social structures, and technological advancements. For example, changes in pottery styles can indicate cultural shifts or interactions between different groups of people. Additionally, the study of pottery sherds can reveal information about cooking and storage practices, as well as dietary habits of ancient societies.

Tools, such as stone implements, metal objects, and bone tools, offer insights into the technological capabilities of past societies. Analysis involves determining the raw materials used, manufacturing techniques, and functional purposes of the tools. The distribution of certain types of tools can indicate specialized activities within a community, such as hunting, farming, or crafting. Changes in tool designs over time can also help trace the evolution of human activities and adaptations to different environments.

Artifacts related to art, such as sculptures, paintings, and carvings, provide glimpses into the symbolic and creative aspects of ancient cultures. Interpretation of art can be challenging, as it often involves decoding the meanings and contexts of symbols and imagery. Artifacts like cave paintings can reveal information about religious practices, mythologies, and the relationship between humans and their environment. By studying art, researchers can gain insights into the aesthetic preferences, cultural values, and beliefs of past societies.

Architectural remains, including building foundations, walls, and structures, offer insights into the built environment and the organization of settlements. Analysis of architecture involves understanding construction techniques, the layout of buildings, and the purpose of different structures within a site. Architecture can provide information about social hierarchies, urban planning, and the economic activities of a society. Temples, palaces, and tombs often hold significance in revealing the religious, political, and elite aspects of a culture.

The interpretation of artifacts goes beyond analyzing individual items. Context is crucial for understanding the significance of artifacts within their original settings. The spatial arrangement of artifacts within a site and their associations with other artifacts can provide insights into daily life, rituals, and activities. Archaeologists also consider the chronology of artifacts to trace changes over time and understand cultural developments.

Artifact analysis often involves collaboration with specialists from various fields. Scientists use techniques like radiocarbon dating, microscopy, and chemical analysis to gain insights into the materials and production methods of artifacts. Cultural anthropologists provide contextual insights by comparing artifacts with ethnographic records of modern societies.

Artifact analysis and interpretation offer a window into the lives of past societies. By studying pottery, tools, art, and architecture, researchers can reconstruct the diverse aspects of ancient cultures, ranging from their daily routines to their spiritual beliefs and technological advancements. This interdisciplinary approach helps create a more comprehensive understanding of human history and cultural evolution.

Archaeologists use a combination of methods and techniques to infer information about societies' social structures, economy, and beliefs from material remains. These material remains include artifacts, architecture, human and animal remains, and other physical traces left behind by past cultures. By studying these remnants, archaeologists can piece together a picture of how societies functioned, interacted, and evolved over time. Here's how they do it:

Artifact Analysis

Artifacts are objects created and used by people in the past. Archaeologists study artifacts to understand aspects of daily life, technology, and economy. For example, the types of tools, pottery styles, and clothing items found can reveal the level of technological advancement, craft specialization, and economic activities within a society.

Stratigraphy

The study of stratigraphy involves analyzing the layers of sediment or soil at a site. Different layers correspond to different time periods. By examining the sequence of these layers and the objects found within them, archaeologists can create a chronological framework for the site and infer changes in social structures, beliefs, and economic practices over time.

Architecture and Urban Planning

The layout of structures within a settlement can provide insights into social hierarchies and organization. Palaces, temples, and monumental architecture might indicate a hierarchical society with distinct social classes. The arrangement of houses, streets, and public spaces can reveal aspects of urban planning and social interactions.

Bioarchaeology

Analysis of human and animal remains, known as bioarchaeology, can shed light on diet, health, migration patterns, and social practices. For instance, the study of skeletal remains can indicate social differentiation (such as status or gender), dietary habits, and evidence of diseases.

Symbolism and Art
Artistic expressions, such as pottery decorations, carvings, and paintings, often carry symbolic meaning. These symbols can provide insights into religious beliefs, social values, and cultural norms. Depictions of deities, rituals, or important events can offer clues about the spiritual and ideological aspects of a society.

Trade and Economy
Analysis of trade goods and their origins can reveal economic connections and networks. The presence of exotic materials or goods can indicate long-distance trade, while the distribution of certain resources can offer clues about local economies and trade routes.

Ethnoarchaeology and Experimental Archaeology
Archaeologists often observe and work with contemporary societies that use traditional technologies and practices similar to those in the past. This approach, known as *ethnoarchaeology*, can provide insights into how certain artifacts were made and used. Experimental archaeology involves recreating ancient techniques and processes to understand how artifacts were produced and how they functioned.

Contextual Analysis
Understanding the context in which artifacts are found is crucial. The spatial relationships between artifacts and other features in a site can reveal their functional and social significance. For instance, items found in a burial context might indicate religious beliefs or social status.

By integrating data from these various sources, archaeologists can construct detailed narratives about societies' social structures, economies, and beliefs. However, it's important to note that archaeological interpretation often involves some degree of speculation, and new discoveries can challenge or reshape existing theories.

The Role of Artifacts Throughout Time

Certainly, artifacts play a crucial role in providing insights into various ancient cultures. Here are case studies showcasing how artifacts have provided insights into the Egyptian, Roman, and Mayan civilizations:

Egyptian Civilization: The Rosetta Stone
The Rosetta Stone, discovered in 1799, proved to be a pivotal artifact for deciphering ancient Egyptian hieroglyphs. This black basalt slab contained inscriptions in three scripts: Greek, Demotic (a script used for everyday purposes), and hieroglyphs. The decipherment of the Rosetta Stone by scholars like Jean-François Champollion in 1822 enabled a deep understanding of ancient Egyptian writing systems and language. This breakthrough unlocked access to countless Egyptian texts, helping

researchers comprehend the society's culture, religion, government, and daily life.

Roman Civilization: Pompeii Artifacts
The city of Pompeii, buried under volcanic ash by the eruption of Mount Vesuvius in 79 AD, provided a unique snapshot of Roman life. Excavations have unearthed artifacts ranging from pottery and frescoes to tools and sculptures. These items offer insights into Roman architecture, fashion, culinary habits, social hierarchies, and even the eruption itself. The casts of human bodies, formed by voids left in the ash as bodies decomposed, reveal the last moments of the inhabitants, offering a poignant look into a tragic event in Roman history.

Maya Civilization: Dresden Codex
The Dresden Codex, one of the few surviving pre-Columbian Maya books, provides valuable insights into Maya culture, astronomy, and religious practices. Dating back to the 11th or 12th century, this hieroglyphic manuscript offers information about the Maya calendar, rituals, and cosmology. Researchers have decoded parts of its intricate calendrical and astronomical calculations, helping us understand the Maya's complex understanding of time and their relationship with celestial events.

Egyptian Civilization: Tutankhamun's Tomb
The discovery of King Tutankhamun's tomb in 1922 by Howard Carter provided an unparalleled glimpse into ancient Egyptian royalty. The tomb contained a vast array of artifacts, including jewelry, furniture, chariots, and even the king's mummified remains. These artifacts shed light on the opulent lifestyle of ancient Egyptian pharaohs, their beliefs about the afterlife, and their artistic and technological achievements. The famous golden mask of Tutankhamun has become an iconic symbol of ancient Egyptian artistry.

Roman Civilization: Vindolanda Tablets
The Vindolanda Tablets, discovered near Hadrian's Wall in modern-day England, consist of wooden writing tablets with inscriptions from the 1st and 2nd centuries AD. These tablets provide insights into the daily life of Roman soldiers stationed in Britain, including correspondence, supply lists, and personal notes. They offer details about military routines, administrative practices, and interactions between soldiers and civilians, enriching our understanding of the Roman military presence in the province.

Maya Civilization: Hieroglyphic Stairway at Copán
The Hieroglyphic Stairway at Copán, Honduras, is a monumental structure adorned with inscriptions that chronicle the history of the city's rulers and their accomplishments. These hieroglyphs and sculptures provide a historical narrative that helps researchers trace the dynastic lineage, political alliances, and significant events in the Maya civilization. The inscriptions on the Hieroglyphic Stairway are crucial in understanding the intricate society and politics of the Maya city-state of Copán.

In each of these case studies, artifacts have played a pivotal role in providing insights into the cultures, beliefs, practices, and histories of these ancient civilizations, allowing us to reconstruct and appreciate their rich legacies.

Chapter 5

Understanding the People

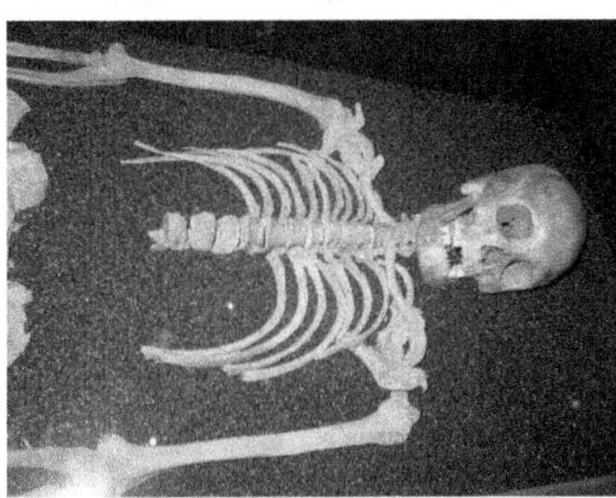

Bioarchaeology is a multidisciplinary field that combines elements of archaeology, anthropology, and biological sciences to study human remains from archaeological contexts. Its primary aim is to understand various aspects of past human populations, including their health, diet, migration patterns, and overall way of life. By analyzing skeletal and dental remains, as well as other bioarchaeological evidence, researchers can gain valuable insights into the lives of individuals and communities that lived long ago.

Bioarchaeologists can assess the health of ancient populations by examining skeletal evidence for signs of disease, trauma, and nutritional deficiencies. For instance, evidence of diseases like tuberculosis, leprosy, and dental cavities can provide insights into the prevalence of certain diseases in the past and their potential impact on human populations. Patterns of skeletal stress markers can also reveal information about the physical demands placed on individuals, such as heavy labor or activities specific to certain occupations.

Human remains can offer crucial information about the diet of ancient populations. The study of dental wear and isotopic analysis of bones and teeth can reveal what types of foods people consumed and whether their diet was primarily based on plant or animal sources. Isotopic analysis, in particular, can help identify the geographical origin of individuals and track changes in diet over time. By understanding dietary habits, researchers can infer aspects of cultural practices, subsistence strategies, and food availability.

Bioarchaeology can shed light on migration patterns and human mobility in the past. Isotopic analysis of human remains can provide information about where individuals were born and where they lived during different stages of their lives. This can help reconstruct migration routes, trade networks, and interactions between different populations. Additionally, the presence of foreign elements in burials or the mixture of skeletal traits from different regions can indicate the movement of people across different geographic areas.

Certain bioarchaeological features, such as burial practices, grave goods, and cranial modifications, can offer insights into social structures and identity in ancient societies. Differences in burial treatment between individuals or groups can indicate social hierarchies, status, and the division of labor. Cultural practices related to body modification or treatment of the dead can reveal important aspects of the group's beliefs and values.

Bioarchaeologists can analyze age-at-death, growth patterns, and evidence of trauma to study the life experiences of individuals from birth to death. This approach, known as life course studies, allows researchers to understand how people's health, diet, and overall well-being changed over their lifetimes.

Bioarchaeology plays a crucial role in reconstructing the lives of past populations by analyzing their skeletal and dental remains. Through the examination of health, diet, migration, and other aspects, researchers can piece together a more comprehensive understanding of human history, shedding light on the complex interactions between societies, environments, and cultures over time.

Ancient DNA (aDNA) is genetic material extracted from ancient remains such as bones, teeth, hair, and other preserved biological materials. The study of ancient DNA has revolutionized our understanding of human history, migration patterns, and relationships between different populations. It has provided valuable insights into the origins, movements, and interactions of past civilizations, as well as the evolutionary history of various species.

The process of extracting and analyzing ancient DNA is challenging due to degradation over time, contamination, and limited sample availability. However, advancements in DNA extraction techniques and sequencing technologies have enabled researchers to overcome many of these challenges.

Ancient DNA extraction involves carefully selecting samples with minimal exposure to modern contaminants. Researchers use techniques that minimize the risk of contamination, often working in specialized cleanroom environments. Fragments of DNA are extracted from the samples, and efforts are made to amplify these fragments for further analysis.

Once the DNA fragments are obtained, they are subjected to high-throughput sequencing methods. These techniques allow researchers to determine the sequence of nucleotide bases in the DNA, which can then be used to compare and analyze genetic information.

Implications for Tracing Ancestry and Relationships

The study of ancient DNA has far-reaching implications for tracing ancestry and relationships among different populations. Ancient DNA has provided critical insights into the movement of human populations across continents and regions. By comparing the genetic signatures of ancient individuals with modern populations, researchers can infer migration patterns and how various groups of humans interacted and interbred.

Ancient DNA can be used to reconstruct family trees and kinship relationships among ancient individuals. This offers a glimpse into social structures, mating patterns, and familial dynamics of past societies. By analyzing ancient DNA from different time periods and geographical locations, researchers can identify the origins of modern populations and how they have evolved over time. Ancient DNA has also revealed instances of interbreeding between different human species, such as Neanderthals and modern humans. This has led to a better understanding of the genetic contributions of these extinct species to the modern human gene pool.

Studying the genetic makeup of ancient populations can shed light on historical trade routes, cultural exchanges, and interactions between civilizations. Ancient DNA can help researchers identify genetic adaptations that allowed ancient populations to survive and thrive in different environments, such as high altitudes or extreme cold.

While the study of ancient DNA has opened up new avenues of knowledge, it also raises ethical considerations. These include respecting the cultural and religious beliefs of descendant communities, obtaining informed consent when possible, and ensuring responsible and transparent communication of findings to the public.

The study of ancient DNA holds great promise for understanding human history, migration, and relationships. By unlocking the genetic secrets of our ancestors, we gain a deeper appreciation of the intricate tapestry of human evolution and the interconnectedness of past and present civilizations.

Studying human remains is a complex and sensitive topic that raises important ethical considerations, particularly when it comes to cultural sensitivity. Here are some key ethical considerations to keep in mind:

Respect for Cultural Beliefs and Practices
Different cultures have varying beliefs and practices surrounding death, burial, and the treatment of human remains. Researchers must be respectful of these cultural sensitivities and seek to understand and adhere to them when studying human remains.

Informed Consent
In cases where human remains are being studied, it's important to consider the wishes of the deceased and their living descendants. Obtaining informed consent from relevant parties, if possible, is essential. This might involve consultation with indigenous communities, families, or relevant religious authorities.

Ownership and Repatriation
Human remains might have cultural, spiritual, and historical significance to certain communities. The issue of repatriation arises when remains have been removed from their original context, often during colonial or unethical practices. Researchers should support efforts to return remains to their rightful cultural communities.

Collaboration and Community Involvement

Engaging with the communities associated with the human remains can foster trust and ensure that research is conducted in a way that aligns with their values. Collaboration with local experts, community leaders, and cultural representatives can help guide the research process.

Sensitive Data Handling

When dealing with human remains, researchers must handle sensitive data and information with care. This includes protecting the privacy and dignity of individuals whose remains are being studied and ensuring that data is not exploited or sensationalized.

Publication and Dissemination

The results of research involving human remains should be communicated in a responsible and respectful manner. Researchers should be mindful of the potential impact of their findings on cultural, religious, and emotional sensitivities.

Educational and Outreach Initiatives

Ethical engagement can extend beyond the research itself. Researchers can contribute positively by engaging in educational initiatives that promote cultural understanding, respect, and awareness of the significance of human remains to different communities.

Balancing Research Objectives

While research into human remains can yield valuable insights into history, genetics, health, and more, these objectives should be balanced with the ethical considerations and cultural sensitivities involved.

Long-Term Storage and Conservation

Ethical considerations extend to the proper storage and conservation of human remains and associated artifacts. Ensuring that remains are treated respectfully and preserved adequately is crucial.

Ethical Review and Oversight

Research involving human remains should undergo rigorous ethical review by institutional review boards (IRBs) or ethics committees. These bodies assess the potential benefits, risks, and cultural implications of the research.

When studying human remains, ethical considerations should guide every stage of the research process. Cultural sensitivity, respect for diverse beliefs, and collaboration with relevant communities are essential to conducting responsible and ethical research in this field.

Chapter 6

Unlocking Mysteries: Decoding Inscriptions

Epigraphy is the scholarly discipline that involves the study of inscriptions, which are written or engraved texts found on various surfaces such as stone, metal, clay, wood, and even textiles. These inscriptions can provide valuable insights into the past, offering glimpses into the cultures, languages, societies, and historical events of ancient civilizations. The field of epigraphy is essential for understanding the evolution of writing systems, languages, and the interactions between different cultures.

Inscriptions and Their Importance

Epigraphy encompasses a wide range of inscriptions, including monumental inscriptions on buildings and monuments, as well as smaller artifacts like coins, pottery, and jewelry. Inscriptions often provide direct and firsthand information about historical events, rulers, religious practices, laws, dedications, and personal achievements.

Epigraphers analyze various writing systems and scripts used throughout history. These include well-known scripts like Egyptian hieroglyphs, Mesopotamian cuneiform, Greek, Latin, Sanskrit, and Chinese characters, as well as lesser-known scripts from cultures worldwide. Some inscriptions are written in scripts that have become extinct or were previously unknown. Epigraphers play a crucial role in deciphering these scripts and translating their content, which can significantly contribute to our understanding of the languages and cultures that used them.

Inscriptions provide valuable cultural context, shedding light on the religious beliefs, social structures, economic activities, and artistic expressions of ancient societies. They offer glimpses into everyday life, customs, and rituals that might not be documented in other historical sources. Epigraphy is an essential tool for dating historical events and establishing chronologies. By examining inscriptions and their associated archaeological contexts, scholars can create more accurate timelines of ancient civilizations.

Different regions and cultures developed unique styles of writing and inscriptions. Studying these variations helps researchers identify cultural influences, trade routes, and interactions between societies. Epigraphy is interdisciplinary, often involving collaboration with historians, linguists, archaeologists, art historians, and specialists in various related fields. This collaboration enhances our understanding of inscriptions and their significance. In modern times, technology has revolutionized the field of epigraphy. High-resolution imaging, digital databases, and 3D modeling have made it easier to document, study, and share inscriptions globally.

Epigraphy is a fascinating field that bridges language, history, archaeology, and art. By deciphering and analyzing inscriptions, epigraphers provide valuable insights into the lives and societies of the past, enriching our understanding of human history and culture. Deciphering ancient scripts has played a crucial role in unlocking historical records and narratives, allowing us to gain insights into the cultures, societies, and events of the past. This process involves decoding languages and scripts that have become obscure or lost over time, and it often requires a combination of linguistic analysis, archaeological evidence, and contextual understanding.

Many ancient civilizations documented their history, beliefs, laws, rituals, and daily life through writing. However, as languages evolve and societies change, these scripts can become unintelligible to subsequent generations. Deciphering these scripts allows us to access a wealth of information that might otherwise have been lost.

Deciphered scripts provide access to historical records that shed light on political events, social structures, economic activities, and cultural practices. For instance, the decipherment of Egyptian hieroglyphs and Mesopotamian cuneiform tablets has revealed details about ancient kings, wars, treaties, religious ceremonies, and even personal stories.

Deciphered scripts enable us to better understand the beliefs, values, and thought processes of past societies. By reading their writings, we can uncover myths, religious texts, literature, and philosophical ideas that were central to their culture. The Rosetta Stone, for example, was crucial in deciphering Egyptian hieroglyphs and provided valuable insights into ancient Egyptian civilization.

Deciphering multiple ancient scripts from different civilizations allows researchers to make cross-comparisons, highlighting similarities and differences between cultures. This can lead to a more comprehensive understanding of historical interactions, trade networks, and the spread of ideas. Many historical mysteries and puzzles have been solved through decipherment. The decipherment of Linear B, an ancient script used in the Mycenaean civilization, revealed a glimpse into the early Greek-speaking world and confirmed the existence of the ancient city of Troy.

Prior to decipherment, historical accounts might have been misinterpreted or misunderstood. Deciphering the Maya script, for example, corrected earlier misconceptions about the Maya civilization and their achievements in mathematics, astronomy, and calendar systems. The decipherment of scripts often enriches historical narratives with personal stories, emotions, and individual perspectives. Documents like letters, diaries, and inscriptions can provide a more intimate view of historical figures and events.

Decipherment goes hand in hand with archaeology, providing context to artifacts, monuments, and structures discovered during excavations. The texts found within tombs, temples, and other sites can help archaeologists reconstruct the purpose and significance of these locations. In essence, deciphering ancient scripts is like piecing together a puzzle of the past. It allows historians, linguists, and archaeologists to reconstruct historical events, cultural practices, and the ways of life of ancient civilizations, enhancing our understanding of human history and our shared heritage.

Notable Examples of Decipherments in History

Rosetta Stone

The Rosetta Stone, discovered in 1799, is a stele inscribed with a decree issued at Memphis in 196 BC during the Ptolemaic dynasty. It contains the same text in three scripts: Ancient Egyptian hieroglyphs, Demotic script, and Ancient Greek. The decipherment was achieved by comparing the known Greek text with the Egyptian scripts, eventually leading to the understanding of Egyptian hieroglyphs. Jean-François Champollion is credited with the successful decipherment in 1822.

Linear B (Mycenaean Greek)

Linear B is an ancient script used for writing Mycenaean Greek, an early form of Greek, on clay tablets primarily in the late Bronze Age. It was first discovered in the early 20th century but remained undeciphered until 1952 when Michael Ventris and John Chadwick successfully deciphered it. The breakthrough came when Ventris proposed that Linear B was a syllabic script, which led to the decipherment of the language and the revelation of insights into the Mycenaean civilization.

Maya Hieroglyphs

The Maya civilization left behind intricate inscriptions on monuments, pottery, and other artifacts, known as Maya hieroglyphs. These glyphs were largely undeciphered until the mid-20th century. Progress was made through the work of various researchers, but it wasn't until the 1970s and 1980s that epigraphers like Linda Schele and David Stuart made significant strides in deciphering the complex script, allowing us to understand Maya history, rituals, and more.

Indus Valley Script

The Indus Valley Civilization, one of the world's oldest urban civilizations, left behind a script that has yet to be fully deciphered. Inscriptions are found on seals, pottery, and other artifacts. Despite extensive efforts, the script remains undeciphered due to the lack of a bilingual text or a known linguistic context, making it one of the most challenging decipherment puzzles.

Ugaritic Cuneiform

Ugaritic is an ancient script used for writing the Ugaritic language, a Semitic language used in the ancient city of Ugarit (modern-day Ras Shamra, Syria). The script was deciphered in the

1930s by French scholar Claude F. A. Schaeffer, leading to a better understanding of the Ugaritic language, literature, and culture.

Linear A (Undeciphered Minoan Script)
Linear A is an ancient script used in the Minoan civilization on the island of Crete. While it's related to Linear B, it remains largely undeciphered, posing a mystery about the Minoan language and culture. Despite extensive efforts, a lack of bilingual texts or a known context has prevented successful decipherment.

These examples showcase the challenges and rewards of deciphering ancient scripts, often requiring a combination of linguistic, historical, and archaeological expertise. Decipherments provide valuable insights into past civilizations, languages, and cultures that would otherwise remain hidden.

Chapter 7

Lost Cities and Forgotten Civilizations

The exploration of archaeological discoveries has played a crucial role in unveiling lost cities and civilizations, offering valuable insights into the history and culture of ancient societies. Here are a few primary examples, in addition to Pompeii, Troy, and Angkor Wat:

Machu Picchu, Peru
Machu Picchu is an iconic Incan citadel located in the Andes Mountains of Peru. It was built in the 15th century and later abandoned, only to be rediscovered by American historian and explorer Hiram Bingham in 1911. The site provides a glimpse into the architectural and engineering prowess of the Inca civilization.

Teotihuacan, Mexico
Teotihuacan is an ancient Mesoamerican city located near modern-day Mexico City. The city thrived between the 1st and 7th centuries AD and is known for its monumental pyramids and impressive urban planning. The civilization that built Teotihuacan remains largely mysterious, but archaeological excavations have revealed intriguing murals, artifacts, and structures.

Palenque, Mexico
Palenque is another Mayan city in Mexico, known for its well-preserved temples and inscriptions. It reached its height during the 7th century AD. The discovery of the tomb of the ruler Pakal the Great in the Temple of the Inscriptions shed light on the religious and political aspects of the Mayan civilization.

Tikal, Guatemala
Tikal is one of the largest ancient Mayan cities and is located in the dense jungles of Guatemala. It was a major political, economic, and cultural center during the Classic Period of the Mayan civilization. The towering temples and ceremonial plazas have provided archaeologists with insights into Mayan architecture, art, and society.

Caral-Supe, Peru
Caral-Supe is considered one of the oldest cities in the Americas, with its roots dating back to around 2600 BC. It is part of the Norte Chico civilization and is known for its complex urban layout, monumental architecture, and advanced agricultural practices. The discovery of

Caral-Supe challenged previous assumptions about the development of civilization in the Americas.

Herculaneum, Italy
Like Pompeii, Herculaneum was a Roman town buried by the eruption of Mount Vesuvius in AD 79. However, Herculaneum is often better preserved due to the unique way it was covered by volcanic materials. The site has provided valuable insights into daily life in a Roman town, including its architecture, art, and even wooden furniture that has survived through the centuries.

Çatalhöyük, Turkey
This Neolithic settlement in Turkey is one of the earliest examples of urban living, dating back to around 7500 BC. The site offers insights into the transition from hunter-gatherer societies to settled agricultural communities. Its distinctive architecture and artifacts provide clues about social organization, religion, and cultural practices.

These archaeological discoveries continue to captivate the world and deepen our understanding of ancient civilizations, shedding light on their achievements, challenges, and contributions to human history. Preserving and studying archaeological and historical sites is crucial for understanding our past, preserving cultural heritage, and informing our present and future. However, these efforts are often accompanied by various challenges that can hinder successful preservation and research. Two significant challenges in this regard are looting and conservation efforts.

Looting, also known as illegal excavation or tomb raiding, involves the unauthorized and often destructive removal of artifacts from archaeological sites. This illicit activity is driven by the demand for valuable antiquities in the black market. Looting not only destroys the context of artifacts, rendering them less valuable for research purposes, but it also leads to the loss of valuable historical information that can only be gathered through careful excavation and analysis. Looting also contributes to the destruction of sites and can lead to irreversible damage to cultural heritage.

Conservation efforts involve maintaining the physical integrity of historical sites and artifacts to ensure their long-term survival. However, effective conservation faces several challenges. Many countries, especially those with numerous historical sites, struggle to allocate sufficient financial and human resources for conservation efforts. This can lead to neglect and deterioration of sites.

Climate change, pollution, and natural disasters can also pose serious threats to historical sites. Rising sea levels, extreme weather events, and changing environmental conditions can accelerate the deterioration of structures and artifacts. Deciding how much and how to restore a site or artifact is also often a complex issue. Over-restoration can erase historical authenticity, while under-restoration might lead to further degradation. Balancing these concerns requires a deep understanding of cultural, historical, and scientific factors.

Sometimes, there's a tension between preservation and development. Economic interests, urban expansion, and infrastructure projects can inadvertently threaten historical sites. Furthermore, conservation and restoration require specialized skills and knowledge. A shortage of trained experts in the field can hamper efforts to effectively preserve and restore sites. Finally, sites that are located in regions affected by conflict, political instability, or social upheaval can be at greater risk of damage and destruction due to lack of protection and enforcement of preservation laws.

Efforts to address these challenges are ongoing. Governments, international organizations, and NGOs are working together to combat looting through stricter regulations, law enforcement, and international cooperation. Conservation efforts are being supported by advancements in technology and scientific techniques, such as 3D modeling, remote sensing, and non-invasive analysis methods. Additionally, raising public awareness about the value of cultural heritage and involving local communities in preservation initiatives can foster a sense of ownership and responsibility for these sites.

The challenges of preserving and studying archaeological and historical sites, including looting and conservation efforts, are complex and multifaceted. Addressing these challenges requires a combination of legal measures, technological advancements, community involvement, and international collaboration to ensure that our cultural heritage is protected for future generations.

Throughout history, there have been several key discoveries that have significantly reshaped our understanding of the past. These discoveries have illuminated new perspectives on human civilization, culture, technology, and even the origins of life on Earth. Unearthing ancient cities like Pompeii, Troy, and Machu Picchu, along with the recovery of artifacts and writings, has allowed us to piece together the daily lives, customs, and advancements of civilizations long gone. These findings offer insights into how societies lived, traded, and interacted with one another, painting a more vivid picture of our collective human heritage.

The discovery of hominid fossils like "Lucy" and the "Homo naledi" remains has revolutionized our understanding of human evolution. By piecing together the puzzle of our ancestors' physical characteristics and behaviors, researchers have been able to construct a timeline of human development and migration patterns over millions of years.

Advances in DNA analysis have allowed us to trace the migratory patterns and genetic heritage of human populations. This has provided insights into our shared ancestry, population movements, and even interbreeding with other hominid species, such as Neanderthals and Denisovans.

Further, exploring the depths of the ocean has led to the discovery of ancient shipwrecks, submerged cities, and unique ecosystems. These findings contribute to our understanding of maritime history, early trade routes, and the effects of climate change on past civilizations.

The completion of the *Human Genome Project* marked a turning point in biology. By identifying and mapping all the genes in human DNA, scientists gained profound insights into genetic variations, hereditary diseases, and the intricate mechanisms that govern human biology. And the discovery of cosmic microwave background radiation provides strong evidence for the Big Bang theory of the universe's origin. This discovery reshaped our understanding of cosmology, leading to the realization that the universe has a finite age and has been expanding since its inception.

Archaeoastronomy is the investigation of ancient structures and alignments that has revealed how various cultures across time and space perceived and interacted with celestial bodies. These discoveries shed light on the significance of astronomical events in shaping religious practices, calendars, and societal organization.

These groundbreaking discoveries collectively underscore the dynamic nature of historical understanding. They remind us that our comprehension of the past is an ongoing process, subject to continuous revision and refinement as new evidence comes to light and novel technologies provide fresh ways of examining ancient artifacts, genetic material, and geological records.

Chapter 8

Archaeology's Legacy and Future: Preserving the Past for the Future

Heritage management involves the preservation, protection, and interpretation of cultural and natural heritage sites, artifacts, and traditions for the benefit of present and future generations. It encompasses a range of activities aimed at safeguarding the tangible and intangible aspects of a society's history, identity, and values. One crucial aspect of heritage management is the role of archaeologists, who play a significant role in preserving cultural sites for future generations.

Heritage management begins with identifying and documenting cultural and natural heritage sites, artifacts, and practices. This involves conducting surveys, research, and documentation to create inventories and databases. Conservation involves maintaining the physical integrity of heritage sites and artifacts, preventing deterioration, and restoring them when necessary. Preservation involves keeping these sites and objects in their present condition to ensure they survive over time.

Restoration involves actively repairing and reconstructing heritage sites to their original state based on historical evidence. Rehabilitation focuses on adapting heritage sites for contemporary use while retaining their cultural significance. Heritage sites are often used as educational tools to teach people about their history and culture. Interpretive programs and displays help visitors understand the context, significance, and stories associated with these sites.

Governments and international organizations establish legal frameworks and regulations to protect heritage sites from destruction, looting, and unauthorized development. Engaging local communities and stakeholders is crucial in heritage management. Their involvement ensures that preservation efforts align with cultural values and community needs.

Archaeologists play a crucial role in heritage management, particularly in preserving cultural sites and artifacts. Archaeologists conduct systematic excavations to uncover artifacts and structures from the past. This process provides insights into the history, lifestyles, and technologies of past societies.

Archaeologists meticulously record their findings through drawings, photographs, notes, and digital documentation. This information is essential for research, interpretation, and future preservation efforts. They then analyze the artifacts and data they collect to understand past human behaviors, social structures, and cultural practices.

Archaeologists additionally collaborate with conservation experts to determine the best strategies for preserving and protecting excavated artifacts and structures. This might involve stabilization, cleaning, and long-term storage. Archaeologists help interpret the significance of heritage sites and artifacts for the public. They create narratives that connect the past to the present, making history more accessible and engaging.

Archaeologists advocate for the protection of heritage sites and educate the public about their importance. They often engage in public outreach, give lectures, and write articles to raise awareness. Archaeologists provide expertise to governments, organizations, and communities in developing policies and strategies for heritage site preservation and sustainable use.

In essence, heritage management and the role of archaeologists are intertwined in their dedication to preserving the tangible and intangible aspects of our collective human heritage for future generations. UNESCO's World Heritage Sites are cultural, natural, or mixed (both cultural and natural) locations around the world that are recognized for their outstanding universal value and are considered to be of immense importance for humanity. These sites are designated and protected by the United Nations Educational, Scientific and Cultural Organization (UNESCO) under the World Heritage Convention, which was adopted in 1972. The primary purpose of this convention is to identify and safeguard sites that hold exceptional cultural, historical, scientific, or ecological significance.

World Heritage Sites play a vital role in preserving and promoting global heritage for several reasons. For instance, World Heritage Sites encompass a wide range of cultural and natural wonders, including historical buildings, archaeological sites, landscapes, ecosystems, and more. By recognizing and protecting these sites, the diversity of human cultures and the planet's ecosystems are preserved for future generations.

These sites serve as valuable educational resources for researchers, students, and the general public. They offer insights into past civilizations, natural processes, and evolutionary history. The conservation efforts and ongoing research at these sites contribute to our understanding of human history, culture, and the environment.

Many World Heritage Sites attract tourists from around the world, boosting local economies and providing employment opportunities. Managed sustainably, tourism can be a source of revenue that supports site conservation and community development.

Further, designation as a World Heritage Site often fosters a sense of pride and identity among local communities. It highlights their unique heritage and encourages efforts to preserve traditions, customs, and historical knowledge. The World Heritage Convention promotes international cooperation by encouraging countries to work together to protect sites that transcend national boundaries. This collaboration can involve sharing expertise, technology, and resources to ensure the effective conservation of these sites.

Many World Heritage Sites have exceptional natural features, such as unique ecosystems, wildlife habitats, or geological formations. By safeguarding these areas, the convention contributes to the protection of biodiversity and the mitigation of climate change.

The designation of a site as a World Heritage Site signifies its outstanding universal value – that is, its significance goes beyond national borders and has importance for all of humanity. This recognition encourages countries to uphold their commitment to preserving these sites for future generations.

Without proper protection and management, many of these sites could be lost due to natural disasters, urban development, pollution, climate change, and other threats. The World Heritage designation brings attention to these risks and encourages efforts to mitigate them.

Overall, UNESCO's World Heritage Sites play a crucial role in preserving the world's cultural and natural heritage. By promoting awareness, collaboration, and responsible stewardship, these sites contribute to the global effort to protect and celebrate the diversity and richness of human civilization and the natural world.

Chapter 9

The Future of Archaeology

The field of archaeology has undergone significant evolution over the years, particularly in terms of interdisciplinary collaborations and advancements in fields like climate science and genetics. This has led to a more comprehensive understanding of human history, cultural development, and the environment.

Climate science has greatly impacted archaeology by providing insights into past environmental conditions. By analyzing climate proxies such as ice cores, sediment layers, and pollen records, researchers can reconstruct ancient climates and their influence on human societies. For example, the study of ice cores from glaciers can provide information about atmospheric conditions, which in turn can reveal patterns of human migration, settlement, and adaptation to changing climates.

Genetic research, particularly ancient DNA analysis, has revolutionized archaeology by offering direct insights into the movements, interactions, and relationships of ancient populations. Through the analysis of skeletal remains, researchers can extract and sequence DNA to study genetic kinship, migration patterns, and even aspects of health and disease in past societies. This has enabled the reconstruction of prehistoric population dynamics and the tracing of ancestry and migrations.

Geoarchaeology is an interdisciplinary field that combines geology and archaeology to understand how landscapes have changed over time and how human activities have impacted them. By examining sediment layers, soil composition, and landforms, researchers can determine how humans utilized and modified their environments. This collaboration helps archaeologists interpret past human behaviors in relation to environmental contexts.

Collaborations with botanical and zoological experts allow archaeologists to analyze ancient plant and animal remains found at archaeological sites. These remains can reveal insights into ancient diets, agriculture, trade, and the relationships between humans and their environment. This information is crucial for understanding the development of agriculture, dietary habits, and the domestication of plants and animals.

Landscape archaeology involves studying the broader spatial context of archaeological sites. This approach combines remote sensing techniques, such as satellite imagery and LiDAR

(Light Detection and Ranging), with traditional fieldwork to uncover hidden archaeological features. By understanding how ancient societies used and transformed landscapes, researchers gain a more holistic perspective on past human behaviors.

The use of digital technologies, such as *Geographic Information Systems* (GIS), 3D modeling, and virtual reality, has transformed how archaeologists record, analyze, and present their findings. These tools enable researchers to create detailed maps, reconstructions, and visualizations of archaeological sites, aiding in the interpretation and communication of complex data.

In recent years, there has been a growing emphasis on collaboration with Indigenous communities in archaeological research. This approach recognizes the importance of incorporating local knowledge and perspectives into archaeological interpretations, fostering a more respectful and inclusive understanding of the past.

The evolving landscape of archaeology is marked by its increasing integration with various scientific disciplines. Interdisciplinary collaborations have enriched our understanding of human history, shedding light on the intricate relationships between societies, cultures, environments, and technologies throughout time.

Archaeology is a field that involves the study of past human societies and cultures through the analysis of artifacts, structures, and other physical remains. While it offers valuable insights into our history, it also raises various ethical considerations, particularly concerning the repatriation of artifacts and the incorporation of indigenous perspectives. Here's a discussion of these ethical considerations:

Repatriation of Artifacts
Repatriation refers to the return of cultural artifacts and human remains to their countries of origin or to indigenous communities. This practice has gained prominence due to concerns about colonialism, exploitation, and the impact of looting.

Cultural Ownership
Many artifacts were taken from their places of origin during colonial times or through unethical practices. Repatriation seeks to address historical injustices by returning these items to their rightful owners or descendants.

Cultural Heritage
Indigenous communities often view artifacts as integral to their cultural identity and spirituality. Repatriation can help restore these connections and provide communities with agency over their heritage.

Preservation
Returning artifacts to their places of origin can facilitate their proper care and preservation within the context of their cultural and environmental surroundings.

Balancing Interests
Ethical debates arise when there are conflicting interests between archaeological research and the rights and desires of indigenous communities. Finding a balance between these interests is a complex challenge.

Indigenous Perspectives
Archaeological research has traditionally been conducted from a Western perspective, often overlooking or disregarding indigenous knowledge and narratives. Ethical considerations in this regard include:

Collaboration and Consultation
Involving indigenous communities in the research process fosters a more equitable partnership and ensures their perspectives are considered.

Decolonization
Efforts to decolonize archaeology involve challenging Eurocentric narratives and methodologies, aiming to incorporate indigenous worldviews and knowledge systems.

Ethical Protocols
Indigenous communities may have specific protocols and beliefs regarding the handling and interpretation of cultural materials. Respecting these protocols is crucial for ethical engagement.

Benefit Sharing
The benefits of archaeological research can extend beyond academia. Ethical considerations involve sharing these benefits with indigenous communities and local populations:

Community Engagement
Archaeologists should engage with local communities and indigenous groups to understand their needs and aspirations, and to ensure that research outcomes have positive impacts.

Capacity Building
Collaborative projects can involve training indigenous community members in archaeological techniques, fostering skills that benefit both preservation efforts and local economies.

Cultural Revival
Archaeological findings can aid in the revival of cultural practices, languages, and traditions that may have been suppressed or lost over time.

The ethical considerations surrounding archaeology emphasize the need for collaboration, respect for indigenous perspectives, repatriation of artifacts, and equitable benefit sharing. These considerations are critical to addressing historical injustices, fostering cultural preservation, and ensuring that archaeological research contributes positively to the well-being of both present and past communities.

Speculating about future discoveries and the role of technology in shaping archaeological research is an exciting endeavor. While no one can predict specific events, one can certainly outline some potential directions and trends based on existing technologies and emerging scientific advancements. Some of the most notable examples are as follows:

Remote Sensing and Aerial Surveys
As remote sensing technology continues to improve, archaeologists will likely use advanced satellites, drones, LiDAR (Light Detection and Ranging), and other techniques to identify archaeological sites and features that are difficult to spot from the ground. LiDAR, in particular, has already proven transformative in uncovering hidden structures beneath dense vegetation.

Virtual Reality and Augmented Reality
These technologies could play a crucial role in recreating past environments and allowing researchers and the public to virtually explore archaeological sites and artifacts. This could enhance the accessibility of archaeological information and aid in the preservation of fragile sites.

Advanced Imaging Techniques
High-resolution 3D scanning, multispectral imaging, and even microscopic analysis could offer deeper insights into artifacts and materials. Analyzing objects at microscopic levels can reveal hidden details, such as faded inscriptions or the composition of ancient pigments.

Artificial Intelligence and Data Analysis
AI could help archaeologists process and analyze vast amounts of data, such as stratigraphic layers, pottery typologies, and architectural styles. Machine learning algorithms could identify patterns and correlations that human researchers might miss, leading to new interpretations and insights.

DNA Analysis
Advancements in ancient DNA analysis could provide insights into the genetic makeup of past populations. This could lead to a better understanding of migration patterns, genetic relationships, and the spread of diseases in ancient times.

Climate and Environmental Reconstruction
Researchers might integrate archaeological data with climate models and environmental data to understand how past civilizations adapted to changing climatic conditions. This could shed light on the interactions between human societies and their environments.

Underwater Archaeology and Deep-Sea Exploration
As technology improves, underwater archaeological research could become more accessible. Advanced diving equipment, remotely operated vehicles (ROVs), and autonomous underwater vehicles (AUVs) could enable the exploration of submerged archaeological sites, potentially revealing insights into ancient maritime civilizations.

Preservation and Conservation
3D printing and advanced materials could play a role in replicating and preserving fragile
artifacts, reducing the need to physically handle originals. Non-invasive conservation techniques
could also improve the long-term preservation of delicate items.

Cultural Heritage Management
Geographic Information Systems (GIS) and digital mapping tools could assist in managing
archaeological sites and heritage preservation efforts, aiding in decision-making and monitoring
the condition of sites over time.

Ethics and Collaboration
As technology continues to shape archaeological research, ethical considerations will become
even more crucial. Issues surrounding cultural sensitivity, repatriation of artifacts, and
collaboration with local communities will need to be carefully navigated.

It's important to note that while these technological advancements hold tremendous
potential, their successful integration into archaeological research will require interdisciplinary
collaboration, ethical considerations, and a balance between embracing innovation and
preserving the integrity of the past. The future of archaeology will likely be a dynamic interplay
between technological innovation and the timeless quest to understand and appreciate our
shared human history.

Conclusion

Archaeology: A Continuing Journey

As we conclude this book, remember that archaeology is an ongoing journey of discovery, where each artifact, inscription, and site tells a unique story about our shared human history. By delving into the past, we not only learn about those who came before us but also gain insights that shape our present and future. May your curiosity about the mysteries of the past continue to fuel your exploration of the fascinating world of archaeology.

The tapestry of human history is woven with countless threads of stories, cultures, and civilizations that have come before us. Archaeology serves as the skilled and dedicated weaver, painstakingly unraveling these threads from the depths of time and bringing them into the light of understanding. Its importance cannot be overstated.

Through the meticulous work of archaeologists, we gain invaluable insights into our past – a past that shapes our present and informs our future. The artifacts they uncover are not mere remnants of a bygone era; they are windows into the lives, aspirations, struggles, and triumphs of those who walked the Earth long before us. They remind us that we are part of an intricate continuum, linked to those who built the foundations upon which our societies now stand.

Archaeology has the power to bridge gaps in our knowledge, to dissolve misconceptions, and to challenge assumptions. It speaks across time and space, connecting us to distant cultures and civilizations, fostering empathy and promoting cultural understanding. By studying ancient ruins, tools, art, and architecture, we gain a deeper appreciation for the incredible diversity of human achievements and the boundless ingenuity that has driven our species forward.

Moreover, archaeology is a testament to the importance of preserving our heritage. As we uncover the relics of our past, we are reminded that the present is fleeting and the tangible remnants of our existence are delicate. The work of preservation is a responsibility we bear for the sake of future generations – to ensure they too have the opportunity to marvel at the wonders of history and learn from the mistakes and accomplishments of those who came before.

In a world where technological advancements sometimes seem to eclipse the wisdom of the past, archaeology anchors us to the roots of our shared humanity. It reminds us that progress is not a linear march forward but a complex interplay of ideas and experiences. By acknowledging the significance of archaeology, we honor the lessons of time and honor the rich tapestry of human existence. So, let us continue to support and champion this noble endeavor, for in doing so, we enrich our understanding of who we are and where we come from.

Glossary

Archaeoastronomy: The investigation of ancient structures and alignments that has revealed how various cultures across time and space perceived and interacted with celestial bodies.

Archaeology: The study of past human cultures and societies through the analysis of material remains such as artifacts, structures, and landscapes.

Biological Anthropology: Biological anthropology, also known as physical anthropology, is a subfield of anthropology that focuses on the biological aspects of human beings, their evolution, variation, and adaptation. It seeks to understand the biological and genetic factors that shape human populations, both past and present.

Climate Science: Climate science has greatly impacted archaeology by providing insights into past environmental conditions.

Consolidation: Strengthening fragile materials using adhesives or consolidants.

Cultural Anthropology: Cultural anthropology is a subfield of anthropology that focuses on the study of human cultures, societies, and their various aspects. Anthropology, in general, is the scientific study of humans, their origins, development, behaviors, beliefs, customs, languages, and social structures. Cultural anthropology specifically delves into the ways people live, interact, and create meaning within their social and cultural contexts.

Dendrochronology: A method that relies on the study of tree rings to establish precise chronological sequences.

Desalination: Removing salts from artifacts like metals and ceramics to prevent corrosion.

Documentation: Recording the conservation process in detail to ensure the integrity of the artifact's history.

Epigraphy: Epigraphy is the study of inscriptions, which are written or engraved texts that are typically found on durable materials like stone, metal, clay, or other hard surfaces.

Ethnoarchaeology: Ethnoarchaeology is a multidisciplinary field that combines elements of archaeology and ethnography to study contemporary and historically recent societies in order to gain insights into the behaviors, practices, and material culture of past societies.

Genetic Research: Particularly ancient DNA analysis, has revolutionized archaeology by offering direct insights into the movements, interactions, and relationships of ancient populations.

Geoarchaeology: An interdisciplinary field that combines geology and archaeology to understand how landscapes have changed over time and how human activities have impacted them.

Geographic Information Systems (GIS): A technology and framework used to gather, manage, analyze, and present geographic or spatial data.

Ground-Penetrating Radar: A geophysical method that uses radar pulses to image the subsurface.

Heritage Management: The preservation, protection, and interpretation of cultural and natural heritage sites, artifacts, and traditions for the benefit of present and future generations.

History: The study of past events and human activities based on written records, documents, and oral traditions.

Humidity Control: Storing artifacts in controlled environments to prevent mold growth, cracking, and warping.

Landscape Archaeology: Studying the broader spatial context of archaeological sites.

LiDAR (Light Detection and Ranging): A remote sensing technology that uses laser light to measure distances and create detailed three-dimensional representations of surfaces and objects.

Linguistic Anthropology: Linguistic anthropology is a subfield of anthropology that focuses on the study of language and its role in human culture, social interactions, and cognitive processes. This discipline examines how language shapes and is shaped by various aspects of human life, including communication, identity, thought, social relationships, and cultural practices.

Looting: The illegal excavation or tomb raiding, involves the unauthorized and often destructive removal of artifacts from archaeological sites.

Radiocarbon Dating: Also known as carbon-14 dating or simply C-14 dating, is a widely used method for determining the age of organic materials.

Repatriation: The return of cultural artifacts and human remains to their countries of origin or to indigenous communities.

Restoration: Actively repairing and reconstructing heritage sites to their original state based on historical evidence.

Seriation: A relative dating method used to order artifacts and other archaeological materials based on changes in style, form, or other characteristics over time.

Stratigraphy: The study of layers of sediment or soil that accumulate over time.

Zooarchaeology: Analyzing animal bones to understand past human interactions with animals, diet, and hunting strategies.

About the Author

Amy N. Koller is a professional archaeologist who presently works and resides in the Midwest. She owns her own archaeological organization, ANK Archaeological Consulting, LLC. She has a Bachelor's degree in Cultural Anthropology and a Master's degree in History. Having grown up in northern Nevada, Amy developed a strong passion for history and archaeology, spending much of her youth wandering the Nevada deserts in search of artifacts related to the past. She has worked on countless archaeological excavations throughout Minnesota and Wisconsin in both prehistoric and historic contexts. Amy is married to her best friend, Jeremiah, and is the mother to their teenage son, Jacen.